BE YOUR TRUE SELF

BY MARIBEL VALDEZ GONZALEZ

CAPSTONE PRESS
a capstone imprint

Published by Capstone Press, an imprint of Capstone
1710 Roe Crest Drive, North Mankato, Minnesota 56003
capstonepub.com

Library of Congress Cataloging-in-Publication Data
Names: Gonzalez, Maribel Valdez, author.
Title: Be your true self / by Maribel Valdez Gonzalez.
Description: North Mankato, Minnesota : Capstone Press, an imprint of Capstone, [2023] | Series: Social justice and you | Includes bibliographical references and index. | Audience: Ages 8-11 | Audience: Grades 4-6 | Summary: "Who are you? How do the identities you hold—like your racial or gender identity—impact you every day? How do they impact others? These big and important questions are key to understanding ourselves. Part of being your true self means learning about group identities and how they affect our experience of the world. With kid-friendly explanations of key ideas and relevant scenarios, this text will help young kids explore their identities and how it shapes their experience"— Provided by publisher.
Identifiers: LCCN 2022001205 (print) | LCCN 2022001206 (ebook) |
ISBN 9781666345537 (hardcover) | ISBN 9781666345551 (paperback) |
ISBN 9781666345568 (pdf) | ISBN 9781666345582 (kindle edition)
Subjects: LCSH: Identity (Psychology) in children—Juvenile literature. | Individual differences in children—Juvenile literature.
Classification: LCC BF723.I56 G66 2023 (print) | LCC BF723.I56 (ebook) | DDC 155.2/2—dc23/eng/20220118
LC record available at https://lccn.loc.gov/2022001205
LC ebook record available at https://lccn.loc.gov/2022001206

Editorial Credits
Editor: Ericka Smith; Designer: Sarah Bennett; Media Researcher: Julie De Adder; Production Specialist: Katy LaVigne

Image Credits
Alamy: Ira Berger, 16, 19, Steve Skjold, 10; Getty Images: Cavan Images, 12, chameleonseye, 17, FatCamera, 6, fstop123, 7, GlobalStock, 5, Glowimages, 28, kali9, 26, Yobro10, 29; Newscom: Eye Ubiquitous, 11; Shutterstock: Bernardo Emanuelle, 14, Brocreative, 21, Franzi, cover, Magnia (background), back cover and throughout, Monkey Business Images, 8, 25, Odua Images, 18, Rittis, 13, wavebreakmedia, 22

All internet sites appearing in back matter were available and accurate when this book was sent to press.

TABLE OF CONTENTS

Words in **bold** are in the glossary.

WHO ARE YOU?

Imagine someone asks you, "Who are you?" What would you say? You'd probably tell them your name. You might tell them where you live. That's a great start! But there are many things that make us who we are. They include our values, our interests, and our identities.

Our identities are things like our **race** and gender. And they impact how we experience the world. We should all be able to be ourselves. And we shouldn't be hurt by others.

An important part of that is learning about our identities. We also need to learn about others' identities. That way we can help make space for all of us to be our true selves.

CHAPTER 1

GROUP IDENTITIES

We all have group identities. They are the social groups we belong to. They include our race, **ethnicity**, gender, and sexual identity. They also include our religion, abilities, and **class**.

Our group identities shape how we view ourselves. But people who share an identity have different experiences. We each have our own mix of identities that help make us who we are.

Learning about group identities helps us understand our experiences. It helps us understand other people's experiences too.

RACE AND ETHNICITY

Our racial and ethnic identities are often a big part of who we are. They help shape our culture. They affect how we see ourselves. And they impact how we are treated by others.

Race is one way we group people. We use physical traits—like skin color—to group people. But racial categories are complicated. Race is an idea people have created—and changed—to benefit certain groups. For that reason, race does have a real impact in our lives. And it affects people who are seen as part of each racial group differently.

In the United States, racial groups now include Indigenous, Black, Asian, and white. Some people might identify with more than one group.

RACISM

Racism is discrimination against a person or a group based on their race. Sometimes, we can see that in the way one person treats another person. But racism often impacts what governments, companies, schools, and other organizations do. We call that institutional racism. For example, a school might have a rule that students cannot wear their hair in dreadlocks. That sort of rule discriminates against Black students.

In the United States, people have used race to justify violence, enslavement, and **discrimination**. This has usually benefited people who are considered white. Racial difference has been used to justify acts like enslaving people from African countries. It has also been used to justify forcing **Indigenous** children to attend schools that strip them of their culture.

Ethnicity is different from race. Ethnicity is more about culture. That includes someone's traditions, language, religion, clothing, and food choices. People with a certain ethnic identity have a shared history in a particular place. Someone's ethnicity might be Igbo. Or it could be Hmong.

A Hmong girl in traditional clothing

Igbo people in Nigeria celebrating the new year

IDEAS IN ACTION

For show and tell, Xochitl (pronounced soh-chee) brings in a picture of her family working in their garden.

"My family grows corn, squash, beans, and tomatoes," she says. "As an Indigneous family, it is important to us that we know where our food comes from."

- **What is Xochitl's racial identity?**

- **How does Xochitl's racial identity influence the way she views food?**

GENDER

Gender is another part of our identity. There are many ways someone might identify. Someone might feel like a girl. Someone might feel like a boy. Or someone might not feel like a girl or a boy. They might identify as **nonbinary**. How someone feels might change too.

When the way a person identifies matches the sex—male or female—they were assigned at birth, they are cisgender. When it doesn't, they are transgender.

FACT Intersectionality is a word that describes how different identities, such as race and gender, work together to shape our experiences. This term was created by Kimberlé Crenshaw, a Black law professor and activist. It helps explain why a Black girl's experience might be different from a white girl's experience and different from a Black boy's experience.

We can show our gender identity by sharing our pronouns. Here are some common pronouns:

- he/him—for people who identify as a boy
- she/her—for people who identify as a girl
- they/them—for people who may not identify as a girl or a boy

Some people use a mix of pronouns, like she/they.

IDEAS IN ACTION

Roxanne is a Black transgender girl. On her first day at a new school, she is nervous about meeting kids who might not understand her gender identity.

When she gets to class, her teacher introduces themselves: "My name is Mx. (pronounced "mix") Thompson. My pronouns are they and them."

Roxanne feels relieved. When it's her turn to introduce herself, she says proudly, "My name is Roxanne. My pronouns are she and her."

- **What is Roxanne's gender identity?**
- **How does her teacher make the classroom a welcoming space for Roxanne?**

SEXUAL IDENTITY

Sexual identity is about who we are romantically attracted to. Some people identify as gay or lesbian. They are attracted to people with the same gender identity. Some people identify as heterosexual. They are attracted to people with the opposite gender identity.

Some people identify as bisexual. They might be attracted to someone with the same gender identity. Or they might be attracted to someone with a different gender identity.

These are just a few of the ways people can describe their sexual identity.

Because there are different ways to love, there are different kinds of families. Some kids might have a mom and a dad. Some might have two moms. And others might have two dads.

Your family may look different from another family. What matters is that a family is centered on love.

RELIGION

Belief systems can also be an important part of our identity. Some people might practice Islam, Hinduism, or Buddhism. Or they might practice Sikhism, Judaism, Christianity, or Earth-based religions. And some might not follow a particular belief system.

Sikh kids dressed for a wedding

A family celebrates Hanukkah, a holiday in Judaism.

Each belief system has its own values and traditions. These values and traditions can shape our community. They can shape what we wear, what we eat, what we do, and what we celebrate. For example, some Buddhists don't eat meat. Some Sikhs wear turbans. And some Christians attend church on Sundays.

Your community or school may recognize some religious practices but not others. Maybe they celebrate Christmas, but they don't recognize **Ramadan**. Ask an adult you trust for things you might need to practice your belief system. Maybe it would help to have a different dress code at school.

Muslim kids learning to read the Koran, the religious text of Islam

FACT A recent study showed that about 31.2 percent of the world's population identified as Christian and about 24.1 percent of people identified as Muslim. About 16 percent of people don't identify with any particular religion.

Hindus praying and meditating

It's also important to be respectful of belief systems that are different from yours. You might share parts of your belief system with others and learn about theirs.

CLASS

Another identity that shapes our lives is our class. The wealth, income, jobs, and education of our family members are all part of our class identity.

In the United States, these things can vary greatly. In a **capitalist** society, resources are not distributed equally. This means that some people have far more money than others.

This impacts what we have, and it impacts what we can do. We might assume things about others based on our experiences. That can impact how we view and treat others. For example, we might think that people's homes are just like ours.

FACT Classism is negative beliefs and attitudes toward people who have less money or education.

But it's important to remember that a person's class status does not determine what a person deserves to have. And it doesn't determine whether someone deserves respect. Different class statuses are the result of a society that's unequal.

ABILITY

We might be born with or develop a disability that affects our body or mind. We might be visually impaired. Or we might need a wheelchair to help us get around.

And we may have different needs from others. We can tell others what we need and don't need. And we might build friendships with people who share our experience living with a disability.

FACT There are different ideas about what language to use to describe people with disabilities. **People-first language** would identify someone as "a person who is deaf." **Identity-first language** would identify someone as "a deaf person." Always ask what language a person prefers.

IDEAS IN ACTION

Dominic is in the sixth grade. He and his friends are talking about joining the football team. Dominic has scoliosis, which means his spine is curved. His doctor recommended he join the cross-country or swimming teams, but not the football team. As Dominic talks with his friends, he starts to feel uncomfortable. His friends assume he will join them on the football team. But they don't know he has scoliosis.

"Actually, I think I am going to try out for the swimming team instead," Dominic says.

"What?! No football? Why not?" asks Simon.

"I can't. I have scoliosis, and it might hurt my back."

"Oh. Well, we'll come to your swim meets if you come to the football games!" Simon replies, smiling.

- **How does Dominic's disability affect this experience with his friends?**

- **How does his friend Simon respond when Dominic tells them about his disability?**

IDENTITY IS POWER

In some communities, certain identities might be considered "normal." That shapes everyone's experience and ideas in a community. It doesn't matter whether they hold that identity.

For example, in the United States, expectations of how to behave or what to value are often based in white culture. Those expectations affect people of color too. They might be different from what they've learned at home.

Those expectations can affect our choices and how we view others. So it's important to understand that what's considered "normal" may be very limited. And we don't need to fit into what's "normal."

Some groups also have more privilege. Privilege is an unearned benefit members of a group have.

For example, nondisabled people have privilege. Restaurants, schools, and offices may not have designed their buildings in a way that includes people with physical disabilities.

When only some identities are viewed as "normal" and experience privilege, it can shape what we believe about ourselves and others. We might not feel valued in our community. Or we might hold a lot of privilege. And we may not have considered others' experiences.

It's important to think about the identities we hold and who has privilege in our communities. We can speak up for ourselves when we may not have privilege. Or we can be more aware of the privilege we have. We can find ways to use it to create a more **inclusive** community.

IDEAS IN ACTION

Marisol is excited to sign up for soccer. She is **Latine**, and when Marisol and her mom approach the table to register for tryouts, the white coach begins asking questions.

"How old is your child?" He speaks loudly and slowly.

"Marisol is twelve," Marisol's mom replies.

The coach then asks loudly and slowly again, "What is your daughter's birth date?"

Marisol notices the coach's tone. "My mom can understand English," she says.

- **Why do you think the coach speaks loudly and slowly?**

- **Why do you think it is important for Marisol to speak up?**

CHAPTER 3
SPACE FOR EVERYONE

We are always learning and growing from our experiences. It's important to honor all our identities. It helps us be our most authentic—or true—selves. It's also important to think about how our identities relate to our daily lives in our community—and the privilege we have.

When we show up as our true selves and we know how our identities relate to others' identities, we can invite others to show up as their true selves too. It's an important step in building meaningful connections with one another.

WHAT IS SOLIDARITY?

Many people are harmed in their daily lives because of their identities. Sometimes it's by someone's words or actions. And sometimes it's by organizations or systems. But there are ways we can support one another. Solidarity is when we help others—with their permission and without asking for anything in return.

We might speak up when we see bullying or protest a school policy that does not consider nonbinary students.

We act in solidarity with others to work toward a common goal of justice for all.

GLOSSARY

capitalist (KA-puh-tuhl-ist)—related to an economic system in which goods and the ways of making them are owned by individuals or companies

class (KLAS)—a group of people in society with a similar way of life or range of income

discrimination (dis-kri-muh-NAY-shuhn)—treating people unfairly because of their identities, like race, gender, or religion

ethnicity (eth-NISS-ih-tee)—an identity marked by a shared history in a particular place; people with the same ethnicity often share cultural practices, language, and belief systems

inclusive (in-KLEW-siv)—including all groups, especially those who have often not been included in the past

Indigenous (in-DIJ-uh-nuss)—belonging to the group of people who first lived in a place

Latine (la-TEE-neh)—from or having ancestors from a country in Latin America, such as the Dominican Republic, Mexico, or Chile

nonbinary (non-BYE-nair-ee)—having a gender identity that is not just boy (man) or girl (woman)

race (RAYSS)—groups into which humans have been divided based on shared physical traits; these broad categories have been created to benefit some groups

Ramadan (RAHM-uh-dahn)—the holy month of the Islamic calendar; Muslims fast from sunrise to sunset during Ramadan

READ MORE

Cherry-Paul, Sonja. *Stamped (For Kids): Racism, Antiracism, and You.* New York: Little, Brown and Company, 2021.

Johnson, Chelsea, LaToya Council, and Carolyn Choi. *IntersectionAllies: We Make Room for All.* New York: Dottir Press, 2019.

Thorn, Theresa. *It Feels Good to Be Yourself: A Book about Gender Identity.* New York: Henry Holt and Company, 2019.

INTERNET SITES

Brittannica Kids: Religion
kids.britannica.com/kids/article/religion/399908

Genderbread Person
genderbread.org

PBS: PBS KIDS Talk About: Race and Racism
pbskids.org/video/dots-spot/3047127185

INDEX

ABOUT THE AUTHOR

Maribel Valdez Gonzalez is an Indigenous Xicana STEM/PBL Coach, former classroom teacher, and consultant. She resides in occupied Duwamish territory, also known as Seattle, Washington. She is from occupied Somi Se'k land, also known as San Antonio, Texas. In her 10 years as an antiracist educator, Maribel has been honored to work with youth and adults to decolonize and humanize teaching practices and belief systems in classrooms and beyond. Maribel's goal is to create academically engaging learning experiences through a culturally sustaining environment that fosters empowerment, healing, and radical kindness. She is also a member of the Antiracist Arts Education Task Force for Visual & Performing Arts in Seattle Public Schools.